Savvy

Picture PERFECT!

Glam Scarves, Belts, Hats and Other Fashion Accessories for All Occasions

by Jennifer Phillips

raintree

a Capstone company — publishers for children

Raintree is an imprint of Capstone Global Library Limited, a company incorporated in
England and Wales having its registered office at 264 Banbury Road, Oxford, OX2 7DY –
Registered company number: 6695582

www.raintree.co.uk
myorders@raintree.co.uk

Text © Capstone Global Library Limited 2016
The moral rights of the proprietor have been asserted.

Edited by Mari Bolte and Alesha Sullivan
Designed by Tracy Davies McCabe
Photos by Karon Dubke
Original photos © Capstone Global Library Limited 2017
Picture Research by Morgan Walters
Production by Kathy McColley
Originated by Capstone Global Library Limited
Printed and bound in China.

ISBN 978 1 4747 2388 6
20 19 18 17 16
10 9 8 7 6 5 4 3 2 1

British Library Cataloguing in Publication Data
A full catalogue record for this book is available from the British Library.

Acknowledgements:
We would like to thank the following for permission to reproduce effects:
Shutterstock: ganpanjanee, design element, Ozerina Anna, design element, Stephanie
Zieber, design element, Vaclav Mach, design element, Yellowj, design element

CONTENTS

Headband hat	**7**
Colourful cadet	**9**
Summery and sporty	**11**
Steampunk style	**13**
Wear it western	**15**
Patchwork wonder	**17**
Band together	**19**
Obi belt	**21**
Comic craze belt	**23**
Fashion meets function belt	**25**
Chunky class	**29**
Tailored for one	**31**
Marvellously mixed up	**33**
Modern art	**35**
Neck charmer	**37**
Funky felting	**39**
Shimmering shawl	**41**
Gauzy glam	**43**
Comfy cargo	**45**
Edgy boho	**47**

YOU'RE one of a kind,

AND YOUR ACCESSORIES SHOULD BE TOO.

Accessories are like spices when it comes to fashion and style. They transform an outfit (and sometimes your mood) in an instant. Hats, scarves and belts do double duty since they are also practical pieces.

The projects in this book let you express individuality and creativity through fashion. Be inspired to add your own twists, making each project uniquely yours.

These must-have creations for every occasion use a range of crafting techniques. While you can use a sewing machine in many of these projects, sewing by hand will work just as well.

SOME PROJECTS INCLUDE ITEMS YOU CAN FIND AT CRAFT OR CHARITY SHOPS. BEYOND THAT, HERE ARE A FEW BASIC SUPPLIES TO HAVE ON HAND:

- *sewing needles in various sizes (sewing machine optional)*
- *thread of various colours and types*
- *scissors*
- *buttons*
- *safety pins*
- *extra-long straight pins*

- *tape measure*
- *seam ripper*
- *embroidery hoop*
- *fabric glue*
- *decoupage glue*
- *craft brushes*
- *utility knife*
- *craft and fabric paint*

Headband HAT

A single headband makes a great accessory. Stack several together to make a slouchy hat that's beyond amazing.

2

MATERIALS:
five fabric headbands
straight pins
needle and thread
felt flowers

1. Decide the order for stacking the headbands. Put the widest one on the bottom.

2. Pin the bottom two headbands together, overlapping by 0.6 centimetres (¼ inch). Whipstitch the pinned edges together. If one band is a little wider than the other, ease the extra fabric into gentle folds as you stitch.

3. Continue pinning and stitching until all the headbands are attached.

4. Make a loose stitch around the top of the hat. Carefully pull the thread tight to cinch the edges and sew them closed.

5. Sew on the felt flowers.

Tip: For an even slouchier hat, add more headbands.

Colourful CADET

Brighten a sombre cadet hat with a stripe of colour! Switch fabrics out weekly for an ever-changing look.

MATERIALS:

tape measure
cadet hat
scissors
fabric
iron
needle and thread
buckle

1. Measure the distance around the outside of your hat. Add 2.5 centimetres (1 inch).

2. Cut a piece of fabric. The length should be equal to your measurement from step 1. The width should be 10.2 centimetres (4 inches).

3. Fold the long edges of the fabric underneath about 0.6 centimetres (¼ inch). Iron the edges so they stay flat, then sew them in place.

4. Wrap the fabric around the hat. Overlap the ends of the fabric. Then hand sew a stitch to one of the fabric ends to attach it to the hat.

5. Stitch the fabric to the hat every few centimetres. Near the front of the hat, slide the buckle onto the fabric. Then continue sewing the fabric to the hat.

Tip: Use loose stitches to hold the fabric in place. This will make it easy to remove when you want to switch patterns.

Summery and SPORTY

Cover a faded hat with fun floral fabric. Vintage prints will add a feminine twist to an old classic.

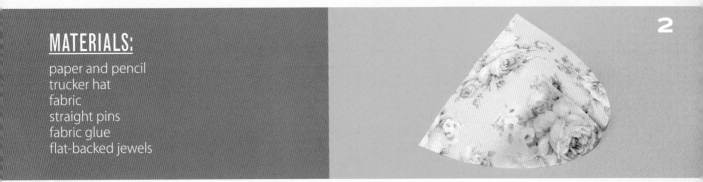

MATERIALS:

paper and pencil
trucker hat
fabric
straight pins
fabric glue
flat-backed jewels

1. Use the paper and pencil to trace the front part of the hat. Cut out.

2. Set the paper template on top of the fabric, and cut out. Add an extra 0.6 centimetres (¼ inch) around the edge.

3. Fold the edges of the fabric in 0.6 centimetres (¼ inch). Pin to the front of the cap.

4. Hand stitch the fabric to the cap.

5. Use fabric glue to decorate the hat with flat-backed jewels. Let the glue dry completely before wearing the hat.

Tip: Instead of jewels, sew on seed beads for a more delicate look. Or go overboard and get crazy with bling!

MATERIALS:

jewellery chain with medium
    or large links
scissors
bowler or top hat
thin ribbon
sewing needle with large eye

thin silver jewellery wire
needle nose pliers
feathers
small metal gears and other
    watch parts
clear fabric glue

Steampunk STYLE

Steampunk fashion is a modern nod to Victorian-era science fiction and the introduction of steam-powered machines. The look mixes historical and futuristic fashion for a creative and stylish combination.

Tip: Rather have the real thing? Find replicas of cameo pendants, charms and gadgets at craft or charity shops. Look for watch parts, gears, washers or anything else that represents steampunk style.

1. Cut jewellery chain to wrap twice around the hat base. Cut ribbon to same length, plus 25.4 centimetres (10 inches).

2. Fold chain in half. Knot the ribbon through the links at one end, leaving 5 centimetres (2 inches) hanging out. Connect the two chain rows by threading ribbon up and down through the links using the sewing needle (if using a thick ribbon, skip some links as you go). Knot the ribbon ends together and slide onto the hat base.

3. Cut two lengths of wire 7.6 to 15.2 centimetres (3 to 6 inches). Use the pliers to twist one end of the wire into a small hook. Continue twisting the wire until you have a spiral.

4. Decide how you want the feathers, gears and watch parts placed. When you're happy with the design, glue them onto the hat. Use the metal pieces to hold the twisted wire from step 3 in place.

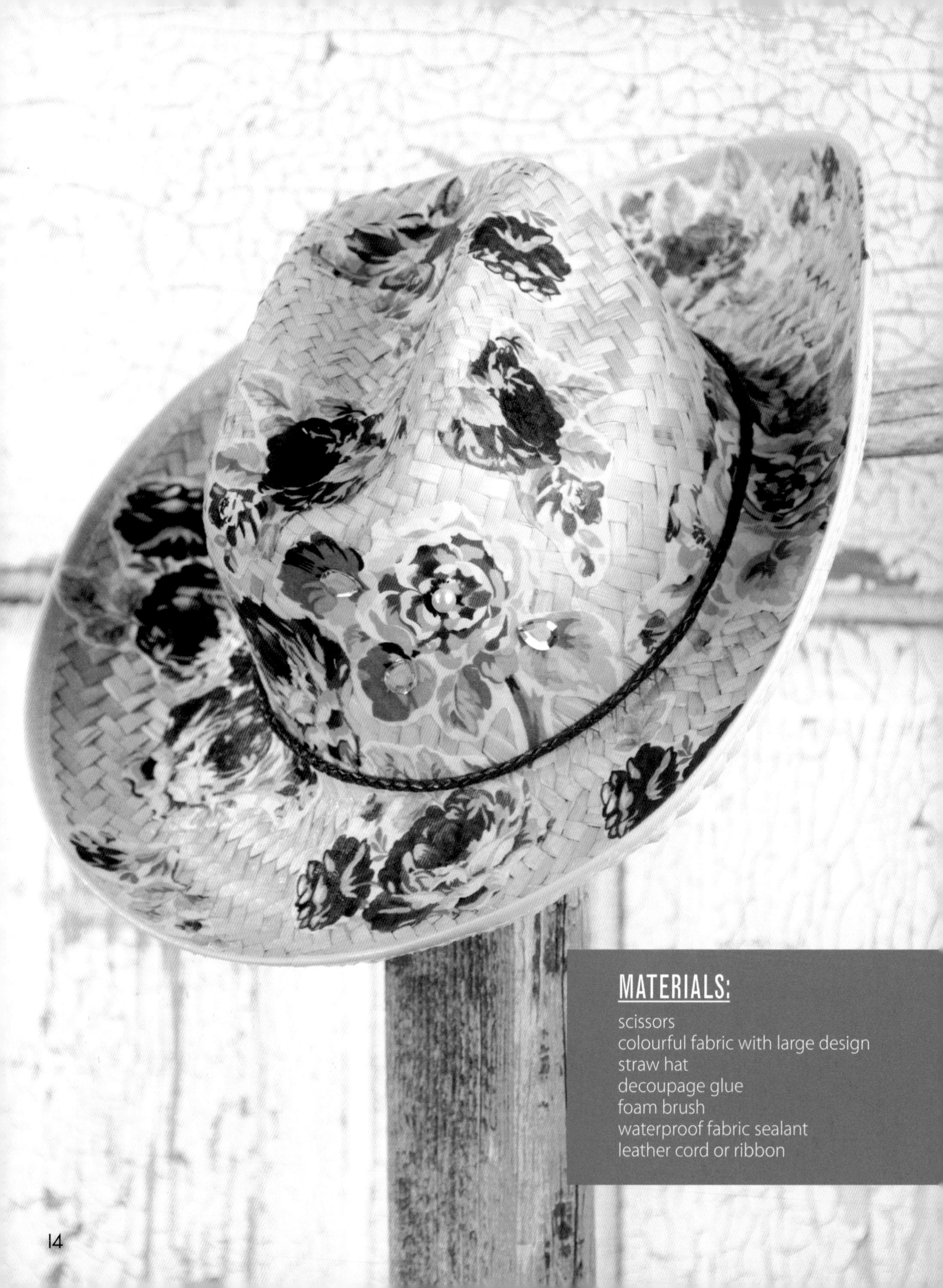

MATERIALS:

scissors
colourful fabric with large design
straw hat
decoupage glue
foam brush
waterproof fabric sealant
leather cord or ribbon

Wear it WESTERN

Are you convinced a cowgirl hat only looks good on the ranch? Think again! With colourful fabric and a little bit of leather, you'll have a fun weekend hat that works anywhere.

5

Tip: If you have a hard time cutting out the designs or your fabric frays a lot, brush the fabric with decoupage and let dry. The decoupage will make the fabric more stiff and easier to cut.

1. Cut the designs out of the fabric.

2. Brush a thin layer of decoupage glue onto the hat and position a fabric design on top. Brush a thin layer of decoupage glue on top of the fabric. Repeat until all of the fabric is attached. Let dry.

3. Place the hat in a well-ventilated area and on a protected work surface. Spray with waterproof sealant. Let dry.

4. Measure the hat's circumference. Cut three pieces of leather cord or ribbon the length of the circumference plus 15.2 centimetres (6 inches).

5. Secure leather or ribbon ends on one side with a knot and make a braid. Fit the braid around the hat base. Overlap the ends and secure with a knot, trimming off any excess.

Patchwork WONDER

Bring out your playful side. Bold strips of canvas and trim add instant fun to a fedora. The more mismatched the look, the better.

MATERIALS:

canvas fabrics in several colors and patterns
scissors
fedora hat
foam brush
fabric glue
decorative ribbon
waterproof fabric sealant
accent piece, such as a button, feather, brooch, pin or flower

Tip: If you don't have a spare fedora, fear not. You can use the same technique on a baseball hat or old straw hat.

1. Cut out fabric strips in varying widths. The strips should all be about 10.2 centimetres (4 inches) long. You should have enough pieces to cover the top of the hat. A typical hat will need about 20 strips.

2. Brush fabric glue onto the hat. Attach strips of fabric to the sides of the hat, and the hat's brim. Fold excess fabric under the brim and glue in place. Work in small sections to keep the glue from getting too dried out.

3. Continue adding fabric strips until the entire hat is covered.

4. Glue ribbon around the hat's brim.

5. In a well-ventilated area, spray with sealant and let dry.

6. Add the accent piece by sewing, pinning or gluing it into place as needed.

MATERIALS:

tape measure
scissors
fabric

sewing machine or needle
and thread
flower embellishment

Band TOGETHER

Take a twist on the traditional turban-style headband with this simple and easy-to-stitch project. Let people get a good look at your pretty profile.

4

Tip: Use any stretchy fabric for this craft, such as fleece, cotton, or lycra. You can also use old T-shirts, swimsuits or blankets.

1. Measure and cut a piece of fabric 15.2 by 56 centimetres (6 inches by 22 inches).

2. Fold the fabric vertically, with the right sides together. Sew the long sides of the fabric together.

3. Repeat steps 1 and 2 to make a second fabric tube.

4. Turn the fabric tubes right-side-out. Fold them in half, and then loop them around each other.

5. Sew the edges of the tubes together. Add embellishment, if desired.

MATERIALS:
felt
two men's ties
chalk
scissors
pins
needle and thread or sewing machine

Obi BELT

Obi is the Japanese word for sash. Put a modern twist on the obi traditionally worn with kimonos. It's a great way to glam up an older outfit.

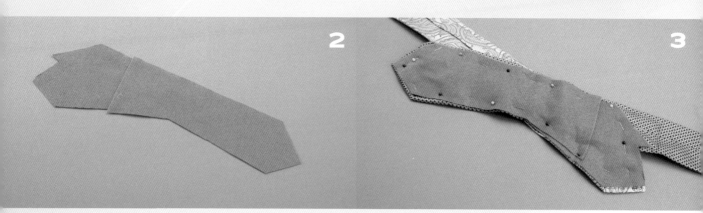

1. Set the felt on your work surface. Lay the ties flat on top of the felt. Overlap the wide ends of the ties, and pin together.

2. Trace the ties' shape from the tips to the edge where they overlap onto the felt. Then cut out the felt.

3. Pin the felt to the back of the ties. Then sew the felt and the ties together. Make sure you sew around the entire felt piece. Remove pins as you sew.

4. To wear, start with the wide end of the ties in the front. Loop the thin ends around your body, and bring them back around to tie a knot in the front.

Tip: Charity shops are great places to find fun ties at bargain prices.

Comic craze BELT

Turn a belt into a statement about your favourite graphic novel, manga or anime heroes. Cut out some comics and get ready to create this perfectly panelled conversation starter.

MATERIALS:
old comic books
leather or vinyl belt
decoupage glue
foam brush
seam ripper

Tip: To add more comic book wearables to your wardrobe, use this technique on other accessories such as shoes and bracelets. Spray shoes with acrylic sealant before wearing.

1. Find and cut out enough images to cover the entire belt.

2. Brush a layer of decoupage glue onto the belt in small sections. Attach paper strips. Let dry.

3. Brush a thin layer of decoupage glue on top of the belt. Let dry.

4. Continue adding layers of decoupage until the belt is as smooth as possible. Let layers dry before adding the next.

5. Use the seam ripper to poke and uncover belt holes.

Fashion meets
FUNCTION BELT

Need a place to store your stuff? With this cute denim belt, complete with hidden pockets, you can leave your bag behind.

3

MATERIALS:

old pair of jeans
scissors
seam ripper
straight pins
sewing machine or
   needle and thread

sticky-back hook and
   loop closures
appliques, metallic
   buttons, studs, or beads
grommets
decorative lace ribbon

1. Cut off both trouser legs and remove seams. Use a seam ripper to remove and keep any cool pockets or decorative details.

2. Measure and cut out a length of jean material that fits around your waist plus 5 centimetres (2 inches). The width should be about 25.4 centimetres (10 inches). You can sew together sections to make a long enough piece if needed. Since jean legs curve in towards the top, you may need to lay the pieces flat and even them out.

3. Fold the material in half lengthwise with the right sides facing in. Whipstitch the short sides.

continued next page

4. Fold down the edges all around the top of the belt to create an inside hem and whipstitch in place. Turn the piece inside out so the right sides show. Sew straight up the short sides of the belt to create pocket dividers.

5. Apply sticky dots at the top of the pockets. Add appliques, decorative buttons, studs or beads.

6. Determine how fitted you want the belt and mark a spot on one end for a fastener hole. Use a seam ripper to create a small hole.

7. Follow package instructions to attach the grommet. Use decorative lace ribbon to tie the belt shut.

Chunky CLASS

Mix book rings and chunky beads for a fun, flexible belt. Pair it with jeans or a cute summer dress.

MATERIALS:

nail polish in several colours

2.5-cm (1-inch) book rings (enough to fit around your waist plus an extra 2.5 cm)

5-cm (2-inch) book ring, or a metal shower ring

short, chunky beads with wide openings

large lobster clasp

Tip: You need beads that will easily slide onto the rings. Look for beads with holes at least 0.6 cm (¼ inch) wide and less than 1.3 cm (½ inch) long. Longer beads will get stuck on the curved rings.

1. Use nail polish to paint the book rings in a variety of colours. Let dry.

2. Add four beads to a 2.5-centimetre ring and snap it closed.

3. String beads onto a second ring. Then attach the two rings. Repeat until the belt is the length you want.

4. When you reach the end of your belt, close it with the 5-centimetre ring. Add beads to the ring but leave 2.5 centimetres without beads so there's space to fasten and unfasten the clasp.

MATERIALS:

tape measure
belt buckle
scissors
fabric
pins

sewing machine or
   needle and thread
iron
seam ripper

Tailored for ONE

Can't find just the right belt in the shop? No worries.
Make your own to match your mood and style.

1. Measure your waist plus 25.4 centimetres (10 inches) for the belt length. Measure the width of the bar in the middle of the belt buckle. Multiply this number by two and add another 2.5 centimetres. This will be the belt's width. Cut out a fabric strip in the dimensions you need.

2. Fold belt in half lengthwise with right sides together. Pin and sew long edge and one short end with a 1.3-centimetre (½-inch) seam. If you are hand sewing, use a backstitch for extra strength.

3. Turn belt right-side-out. Use an iron to flatten the belt.

4. Use the seam ripper to cut a small centred hole 3.8 centimetres (1.5 inches) below the edge of the open short end. Sew a tight buttonhole stitch around the hole to keep the edges from fraying.

5. Put a horizontal tacking stitch 0.6-centimetres (¼-inch) below this same open edge.

6. Slip the end with the tacking stitch through the buckle. Insert the buckle prong through the belt hole. The prong should lay flat, pointing out from the end of the belt.

7. Turn the belt over and fold under the end fabric at the tacking stitch. Whip stitch the fold in place. Remove the tacking stitch.

8. Try on the belt and mark where you want more belt holes to go. Repeat the steps to add more buttonhole-stitched openings.

Tip: Belt buckle feel too bare? Wrap it with yarn! Tie one end of the yarn to the buckle. Then wrap the yarn, tying where necessary. When done, trim off the extra pieces around any knots, push the knots to the underside and use a little craft glue to secure any ends.

MATERIALS:

- tape measure
- scissors
- fabric remnants
- narrow plain scarf
- fabric spray adhesive
- ric rac ribbon
- fabric glue

Marvellously MIXED UP

Need a no-sew way to dress up a plain winter scarf?
Pick a colour theme or a kaleidoscope of colour to
create your one-of-a-kind look.

1. Measure and cut enough small fabric squares to cover the entire scarf. You'll want at least two squares for each row.

2. Lay the scarf flat on a protected surface. Plan your design and arrange the squares.

3. Spray fabric adhesive on the scarf. Quickly place squares on top of the sticky surface. Let dry.

4. Cut two lengths of ric rac for each edge. Cut additional pieces to cover the fabric square's edges.

5. Glue ric rac to cover all square edges. Let the glue dry completely before wearing your scarf.

Tip: For a look that's longer lasting, sew on the patches using a backstitch.

Modern ART

Want a way to show off your artistic side?
Sometimes the best art isn't hung on the wall.

MATERIALS:

pinking shears
medium-weight jersey
  knit fabric
tape measure
straight pins
stencils
fabric paint and brushes
fabric glue
tweezers
sequins
small seed beads
felt or fabric flowers
needle and thread
ribbon or lace

Tip: Don't have pinking shears? You can either leave the scarf edges unfinished or sew a narrow hem.

1. Use pinking shears to cut fabric to 30.5 by 152.4 centimetres (12 by 60 inches).

2. Measure 35.6 centimetres (14 inches) from the short edges and mark with straight pins.

3. Place a stencil on the fabric and brush on paint. Use different stencils and paints to add a variety of images on both bottom sections of the scarf. Let dry.

4. Squeeze a thin layer of glue onto one of the shapes. Use tweezers to attach sequins or beads. Add flowers; attach with a few stitches for extra stability. Let glue dry.

5. Glue the ribbon or lace to the ends of the scarf.

MATERIALS:

plain T-shirt (adult large
 or extra large)
20.3 cm (8 inch)
 paper plate
scissors

split key ring paper tags
small pictures
decoupage glue
paintbrush
pencil

Neck CHARMER

Ordinary becomes extraordinary as you transform a T-shirt
and office supplies into a personalized fashion statement.
Add scarf charms showcasing your interests.

FOR THE SCARF:

1. Lay T-shirt flat. Use the paper plate as a tracing template to cut out as many circles as you can. Save the sleeves.

2. Turn a T-shirt circle into a spiral by cutting into the outside edge. Slowly curve the cuts inwards until you reach the circle's centre. You should have a long, spiralled strip of fabric. The narrower the strip is cut, the longer the strand will be.

3. Repeat with each circle, cutting strips in different widths for variety.

4. Arrange the spiral strips into a row. Trim a hemmed cuff from the shirt sleeve and tie the cuff around the strips in the middle.

FOR THE CHARMS:

1. Remove the wire ring from the tags. Trim your picture to fit the tag circle.

2. Brush decoupage glue onto the tag. Attach the image and brush another layer of glue over the top. Let dry.

3. Turn the tag over and repeat step 2.

4. Use a pencil to poke a small hole in the key tag. Reattach the wire ring. Slide fabric between the key tag rings.

*Tip: Print photos in the size you need, or look through
magazines to find small pictures to use.*

Funky FELTING

Re-use old jumpers to experiment with colour blocking!
Create a fun geometric look that will have you looking
forward to a frosty forecast.

MATERIALS:
old woollen jumpers
    in various colours
netted laundry bag
scissors
needle and thread

Tip: Not into squares or hexagons? Make
stencils in the shapes of quatrefoils,
chevrons or any other fun design. Sew on
beads or jewels for some sparkle.

1. Felt the jumpers first so they won't unravel. Put them in a netted bag and wash in hot water (no detergent needed). Spread the wet jumpers flat on towels to air dry.

2. Cut a scarf piece from one of the jumpers. Cut from a bottom hem over the jumper's shoulders to the hem on the other side of the jumper. Or you can cut around the jumper's torso in a spiral shape.

3. Cut out pieces of various shapes from the other jumpers. Squares, triangles and hexagons are a few ideas. Cut additional smaller pieces in those same shapes, varying colours and tones.

4. Stitch the layered pieces together, starting with the largest and working your way to the smallest.

5. Sew the felt pieces onto the scarf.

Shimmering SHAWL

A chilly night calls for a lightweight wrap. Delicate tulle flowers turn flowy fabric into a shawl that's both pretty and practical.

MATERIALS:

lightweight fabric
scissors
needle and thread
3 inch (7.6 cm) circle stencil

burgundy tulle
gold tulle
buttons or beads
fabric glue

3

1. Cut fabric 81.3 by 127 centimetres (32 by 50 inches) to make the shawl. Hem the sides using a small straight stitch.

2. Use the stencil to cut out 24 circles from the burgundy tulle. Cut out 12 circles from the gold tulle.

3. Layer two burgundy circles on top of one gold circle. Pinch in the middle to create a flower shape. Whipstitch the pinched bottom section together. Use your fingers to flatten and shape the flower.

4. Repeat step 3 to make 12 flowers.

5. Glue beads or buttons to the centre of each flower. Let dry.

6. Attach flowers along the edges of the shawl with the fabric glue. Add small stitches to reinforce, if desired.

Tip: Make as many or as few flowers as you want. A shawl covered with hundreds of flowers would make a huge impact!

Gauzy GLAM

Dream up a fanciful, lightweight summer covering with cheesecloth and fabric dye. Use an ombre technique to produce a gradual colour shift from light to dark.

MATERIALS:

cheesecloth
fabric dye
small spray bottle
salt
hanger
dust sheet or old newspaper

Tip: Adding salt to the dye helps to keep the scarf's colours from washing away or getting onto other clothes. Handwashing is best, but use a delicate cycle if you toss it in the washing machine.

1. Cut a piece of cheesecloth about 35.6 by 160 centimetres (14 by 63 inches). Drape it on a hanger and carefully place it on the drop cloth.

2. Mix two capfuls of liquid dye and 15 millilitres (one tablespoon) of salt in the spray bottle. Fill the rest of the way with hot water.

3. To create an ombre pattern, spritz the fabric at least 8 centimetres away for the sections where you want a lighter colour. Move closer and spray more heavily to make the colour gradually darker. The fabric should be soaked, especially where you want the heaviest shade.

4. Let the scarf air dry on the dust sheet until it is slightly damp. Hang it up to finish drying.

MATERIALS:
flannel shirt with chest pockets (adult size)
scissors
sewing needle and thread
lace or trim

Comfy CARGO

On the go but no place to store your stuff? Turn an old flannel shirt into a handy scarf. The four pockets are tailor-made for weekend outings.

7

Tip: Chambray or corduroy shirts also work well for this project.

1. Cut out the front and back sections of the flannel shirt. Remove the chest pockets without cutting into the front section of the shirt.

2. Fold the back section in half lengthwise. Cut along the fold. Trim off any curved parts to make straight edges.

3. Put right sides together and stitch short edges to create a long scarf.

4. Cut the shirt's front to create two large pockets that are 30.5 centimetres (12 inches) long and as wide as the scarf.

5. Use a straight stitch to sew the small chest pockets onto the top middle of each large pocket section.

6. Pin and sew the large pocket sections to the back side of the scarf's bottom edges, using a whipstitch. Turn out the pockets so the seams are on the inside and the pockets now show on the scarf's front.

7. Fold the unfinished long edges of the scarf underneath twice and hem.

8. Sew lace or trim along the top edges of the large pockets.

MATERIALS:

decorative paper
scissors
ruler
glue stick
skewer

coloured ribbons
yarn
binder clip
needle and thread

Edgy BOHO

From long skirts to beaded bangles, Boho style is here to stay. Create your own whimsical look with a colourful scarf that's all your own.

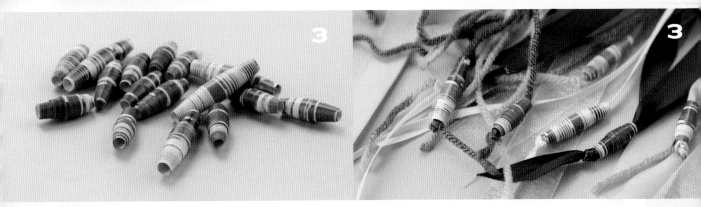

FOR THE BEADS:

1. Cut a triangle from the paper 25.4 centimetres (10 inches) long and 2.5 centimetres (1 inch) across at its widest point.

2. Lay triangle flat, pattern side down. Apply glue to the back.

3. Starting with the widest end, roll the paper around the skewer to make a bead. Slide the paper bead off the skewer to dry.

4. Repeat steps 1–3 to make 16 beads.

FOR THE SCARF:

1. Cut ribbons and yarn into 152.4-centimetre (60-inch) pieces. Arrange strands to form your scarf. Use a binder clip to hold the strips place.

2. Use needle and thread to tie the ribbons and yarn together in the centre.

3. String beads onto the ribbons and yarn, knotting the ends to keep the beads from sliding off.

Tip: Add a little extra sparkle by adding glitter or glow in the dark craft paint to your beads. Make a few extra beads to create a matching necklace or bracelet.

Find out more

Accessories for All (Be Creative), Anna Claybourne (Franklin Watts, 2015)

I Can Make My Own Accessories, Georgia Vaux and Louise Scott-Smith
(Thames & Hudson, 2016)

Maker Projects for Kids Who Love Fashion, Sarah Levete
(Crabtree Publishing, 2016)

About the author

Jennifer Phillips dabbles in all things crafty, influenced by her childhood years with
an artist for a mum who loved experimenting with materials and methods. Jennifer
lives in Seattle, Washington, USA. She likes to write about artists and crafting when
not working on her own projects.

Books in this series: